C0-APO-044

WITHDRAWN

TE

UNIVERSITY SCHOOL LIBRARY
UNIVERSITY OF WYOMING

DODD, MEAD WONDERS BOOKS

WONDERS OF ALLIGATORS AND CROCODILES by Wyatt Blassingame
WONDERS OF ANIMAL ARCHITECTURE by Sigmund A. Lavine
WONDERS OF ANIMAL NURSERIES by Jacquelyn Berrill
WONDERS OF BARNACLES by Arnold Ross and William K. Emerson
WONDERS OF THE BAT WORLD by Sigmund A. Lavine
WONDERS BEYOND THE SOLAR SYSTEM by Rocco Feravolo
WONDERS OF THE BISON WORLD by Sigmund A. Lavine and Vincent Scuro
WONDERS OF THE CACTUS WORLD by Sigmund A. Lavine
WONDERS OF CARIBOU by Jim Rearden
WONDERS OF THE DINOSAUR WORLD by William H. Matthews III
WONDERS OF THE EAGLE WORLD by Sigmund A. Lavine
WONDERS OF THE FLY WORLD by Sigmund A. Lavine
WONDERS OF FROGS AND TOADS by Wyatt Blassingame
WONDERS OF GEESE AND SWANS by Thomas D. Fegely
WONDERS OF GEMS by Richard M. Pearl
WONDERS OF GRAVITY by Rocco Feravolo
WONDERS OF THE HAWK WORLD by Sigmund A. Lavine
WONDERS OF HERBS by Sigmund A. Lavine
WONDERS OF HUMMINGBIRDS by Hilda Simon
WONDERS OF THE KELP FOREST by Joseph E. Brown
WONDERS OF MATHEMATICS by Rocco Feravolo
WONDERS OF MEASUREMENT by Owen S. Lieberg
WONDERS OF THE MONKEY WORLD by Jacquelyn Berrill
WONDERS OF THE MOSQUITO WORLD by Phil Ault
WONDERS OF THE OWL WORLD by Sigmund A. Lavine
WONDERS OF THE PELICAN WORLD by Joseph J. Cook and Ralph W. Schreiber
WONDERS OF PRAIRIE DOGS by G. Earl Chace
WONDERS OF ROCKS AND MINERALS by Richard M. Pearl
WONDERS OF SAND by Christie McFall
WONDERS OF SEA GULLS by Elizabeth Anne and Ralph W. Schreiber
WONDERS OF SEALS AND SEA LIONS by Joseph E. Brown
WONDERS OF SOUND by Rocco Feravolo
WONDERS OF THE SPIDER WORLD by Sigmund A. Lavine
WONDERS OF SPONGES by Morris K. Jacobson and Rosemary K. Pang
WONDERS OF STONES by Christie McFall
WONDERS OF THE TREE WORLD by Margaret Cosgrove
WONDERS OF THE TURTLE WORLD by Wyatt Blassingame
WONDERS OF WILD DUCKS by Thomas D. Fegely
WONDERS OF THE WOODS AND DESERT AT NIGHT by Jacquelyn Berrill
WONDERS OF THE WORLD OF THE ALBATROSS by Harvey I. and
   Mildred L. Fisher
WONDERS OF THE WORLD OF BEARS by Bernadine Bailey
WONDERS OF THE WORLD OF HORSES by Sigmund A. Lavine and Brigid Casey
WONDERS OF THE WORLD OF SHELLS by Morris K. Jacobson and
   William K. Emerson
WONDERS OF THE WORLD OF WOLVES by Jacquelyn Berrill
WONDERS OF YOUR SENSES by Margaret Cosgrove

599
Bro

$3.71
14255

Wonders of
Seals and Sea Lions

JOSEPH E. BROWN

Illustrated with photographs

DODD, MEAD & COMPANY · New York

UNIVERSITY SCHOOL LIBRARY
UNIVERSITY OF WYOMING

For Erik

Illustration Credits

Joseph E. Brown, 2, 6, 10, 17, 18, 27, 28, 29, 31, 32, 36, 40, 41, 57, 64; Anne Ensign, 12; Naval Undersea Center, 34, 67, 69, 70, 71; Sea World, 9, 16, 21, 23, 47, 49, 50, 52, 53, 54, 59, 61, 62, 63.

Copyright © 1976 by Joseph E. Brown
All rights reserved
No part of this book may be reproduced in any form
without permission in writing from the publisher
Printed in the United States of America

Library of Congress Cataloging in Publication Data

Brown, Joseph E   1929-
    Wonders of seals and sea lions.

    Includes index.
    SUMMARY: Discusses the characteristics and habits
of seals and sea lions.
        1.   Seals (Animals)—Juvenile literature.   2.   Sea
lions—Juvenile literature.   [1.   Seals (Animals)
2.   Sea lions]   I.   Title.
QL737.P64B76   599'.745   76-14878
ISBN 0-396-07344-1

Contents

Seals and sea lions have bodies which are adapted for swimming.

1. What Is a Pinniped?

Long before man appeared on earth, a group of animals began to leave the dry land of the continents and return to the sea where all life began. This process took a long time—millions of years, in fact.

At first, they merely nibbled food at the oceans' edges, or waded into shallow water, remaining on the land the rest of the time. But over the years, the face of the earth itself began to change and the land animals found themselves forced to depend more and more upon the sea or perish.

As the oceans' waters rose higher on the coastlines of the continents and later swept over entire land masses, many of the animals ventured farther out into the sea to seek their food. As they did, their bodies slowly changed from generation to generation so that they were able to move about more in their new environment. Feet which had been used for walking, digging, or climbing on the land became useless in the sea. During the long process of evolution, they became flippers and flukes instead which could be used for propulsion. Because water is more resistant than air, their bodies became more streamlined, which made swimming easier. Senses such as hearing, sight, and smell slowly changed so the animals could more easily hunt food in an environment where visibility was poorer than on the land.

7

Soon, the animals were spending most of their lives in the water. All told, it took nature about 100 million years to transform the land mammals into the marine mammals that we recognize in the sea today. The earliest of four major groups to to make the transition were the cetaceans—the whales and porpoises. Their feet disappeared entirely, becoming flippers and flukes used for propulsion.

The sirenians came next, starting about 80 million years ago. They are the plant-eating dugongs and manatees we know today. The most recent marine mammals in this evolutionary cycle are the sea otters, which began to enter the sea about two million years ago. Although their hind feet have become flippers, their front feet are still very much like those of land animals.

Much nearer the middle of the 100 million-year distance in time were the seals, sea lions, and walruses. Because they began the land-to-sea transition about midway in the time span, they are perhaps the most remarkably adapted of the four groups to *both* land and ocean environments.

Depending upon their species, seals and sea lions spend a great deal of the year on land where their flippers help them move about, even if this is accomplished somewhat awkwardly. Whales are bound to the sea and cannot move about on land at all, while the more recent sea otters are quite adept at doing so.

It is on the land that female seals and sea lions give birth to their young, where mating takes place, and where they sleep. (However, the Alaskan fur seal can sleep equally as well in the water.) But even the young seals and sea lions instinctively learn to swim and forage about for food in the ocean depths not long after they are born. All seals are accomplished swimmers and divers and can remain submerged for long periods of time. Yet they have bone structures basically the same as land mammals.

As we have seen, all four groups of these animals are *mammals*. All mammals have certain features in common. They are all warm-blooded air-breathers that have backbones composed of *vertebrae*. Their bodies are covered with hair or fur. They give birth to their young live, rather than by laying eggs. And female mammals nurse their babies on milk developed within their bodies.

Man is a mammal. So is the rhinoceros, the cow, and the dog. There are about four thousand species of mammals altogether, so many that scientists have further divided them into nineteen groups or *orders*. One of them is the order Carnivora, which consists of the mammals that are flesh- or meat-eaters as opposed to those that eat plants. The carnivores are again divided into two suborders. One is the Fissipedia, which includes cats, dogs, bears, weasels, sea otters, and a number of other animals. With the exception of the sea otter, all are land mammals. Seals, sea lions, and walruses fall into the second suborder, Pinnipedia, which means "fin-footed." (Some scientists, however, consider the pinnipeds as a separate order of mammals and not a suborder of the carnivores.)

Within the Pinnipedia are three further groupings called *families*. The largest number of species among the pinnipeds—

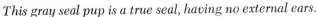

This gray seal pup is a true seal, having no external ears.

eighteen altogether—is found in the family Phocidae. They are referred to either as "true" or "earless" seals, distinguished by the fact that they have no external ears, only tiny openings in their heads.

Pinnipeds with external ears are grouped in the family Otariidae. Numbering thirteen species altogether, they include the fur seals and sea lions. (In common usage, many people refer to all pinnipeds except the walrus simply as "seals." This word will be used from time to time in this book when referring to members of both the Phocidae and Otariidae families.)

Walruses are also pinnipeds. Their two closely related species belong to the family Odobenidae. They might be called cousins of the seals and sea lions.

Although scientists separate seals and sea lions into families partly on the basis of the structure of their ears, there are other

Sea lions have external ears.

An old print showing the pinnipeds—walrus, sea lion, and seals.

ways to tell the difference. Members of the family Otariidae (fur seals and sea lions, the otarids) are able to move about on the land better than true seals because they have larger front flip-

Sealion

Hind Flipper

Front Flipper

True Seal

Front Flipper

Hind Flipper

The flippers of sea lions and true seals differ.

pers. On land, true seals (the phocids) cannot "walk" like the otarids because they have smaller flippers. They move instead by wiggling their entire bodies, something like the caterpillar. Because of these differences, the otarids and phocids sometimes are divided as "walkers" and "crawlers."

If you look closely at the front flippers of both seals and sea lions, you will find that each contains five "fingers," left over from the days when they walked about as land mammals. Those on the sea lions are covered with more skin than those of the true seals. On seals, the flippers look like gloved hands, with five fingernails protruding. The rear flippers are easily recognized as five-toed feet which are webbed, with large and small toes elongated.

Pinnipeds are found in all parts of the world. Their total population is estimated at about 20 million. The majority live in the cold waters of the Arctic and Antarctic, although some are found in temperate and even subtropic waters. As with any warm-blooded animals that spend long periods in the water, pinnipeds have been given an insulation system that protects them from the cold.

Nature has insulated them in two basic ways. One is a covering of hair. On land, this prevents the loss of body heat by trapping an insulating layer of air next to the skin. The hair on fur seals, which live in the coldest climates, is especially long and thick and is grown in two distinct layers. As a second means of protection, all pinnipeds have a thick layer of fat under their skin, called blubber. Because the thickness of both blubber and hair varies from species to species, scientists use these as still another means of grouping seals and sea lions into families and subfamilies.

Although scientists only fairly recently began to make serious studies of seals, the animals themselves have long fascinated humans. During different periods of history, they were given

13

various names such as sea dogs, sea wolves, and sea bears, and many legends developed around them.

In some countries, seals were affectionately regarded as almost human-like. In the Hebrides Island off the west coast of Scotland, for instance, legends once persisted that gray seals assumed human form at will and that human men married "seal women." According to one of these Scottish fables, seals talked and sang, saved the lives of lost fishermen, and warned of approaching storms and other dangers.

Possibly the reason for many of the stories is that seals in many ways *do* remind us of our fellow humans. Humans tend to regard mammals higher among the animals partly because of their high level of intelligence. Seals in the sea are playful and often they "perform" for humans without having to be rewarded, a trait by which many scientists measure intelligence levels.

In the ocean, too, the heads of seals and sea lions often have been mistaken for those of humans, mainly because of their human-like whiskers.

Seals are still linked with the land, much more so than the whales and porpoises, but less than the sea otters that began the seaward return later. In common with other mammals, seals cannot breathe underwater, since they do not have gills as fish do. In many other ways, they share many characteristics with land mammals; they merely *adapted*, or changed, for life in the oceans.

In another several million years of evolutionary adaptation, perhaps, they will give up more of their ties with the land and become even more dependent upon the sea as have the earlier-arriving cetaceans.

2. More About Seals

What did the pinnipeds look like before they ventured into the sea millions of years ago? No one really knows for certain, since seals and sea lions left no fossil records of their earliest land-to-sea transition. Fossils are hardened remains of animal or plant life left in the earth's crust. By closely examining them, scientists can guess with considerable accuracy at what an animal looked like before it began to adapt to a new environment, in the case of the pinnipeds, the sea.

Some scientists believe that because of the marked differences in their bodies, the phocids (the "crawlers") and the otarids (the "walkers") evolved from different land animal ancestors. Others suggest that they had a common ancestor, probably the same animal that became today's weasel, dog, or bear.

Whatever their origin millions of years ago, the seals and sea lions of today have much in common, although their food, habits, and physical characteristics vary greatly from species to species.

For instance, the smallest of the pinnipeds, the ringed seal of the North Polar region, measures only five feet from nose to tip of tail, and weighs but 250 pounds, while his mammoth cousin, the well-named elephant seal, often weighs up to four tons and reaches twenty feet in length.

Seals are very social animals. With the possible exception of

A 2000-year-old fossilized "mummy" of a crabeater seal found in Antarctica.

UNIVERSITY SCHOOL LIBRARY
UNIVERSITY OF WYOMING

the leopard seal of Antarctica, about which very little is known, they rarely are seen alone. They seem to love to frolic together in the sea, sometimes inventing their own "games," tumbling about underwater, exploring everything in sight with cautious curiosity.

They call to each other almost constantly, their voices ranging from the high-pitched bleats of the young to the loud roar and barking of the adults.

Some seals live in large herds. Others congregate in smaller ones. While many roam great distances in herd migrations, there are others that seldom leave their colonies or *rookeries* the year around. Whether they migrate depends to some extent upon the climate where the colonies are located. The migratory instinct is particularly uncanny in the Alaskan (or northern) fur

A group of sea lions playing in the water.

Two California sea lions vocalizing.

seals. Most of them leave and then return to the same breeding sites in the Pribilof Islands of the Arctic in a round-trip seasonal journey exceeding 8,000 miles.

Very often, the colonies to which they return are those of their own birth. Because for a part of the year seals are dispersed over thousands of miles of ocean, nature has given the seal this homing instinct so that it can be with its own kind during the time of year when the cycle of breeding and birth begins anew.

Generally speaking, the colonies are located on islands far from mainland coasts, on ice floes, or on points of land remote from man and animal predators.

Seal family life is much different from that of human families. It consists of a single male (or *bull*) and several females (*cows*) gathered in a *harem*, which the bull defends fiercely against other males.

Especially among the larger pinnipeds, such as the Steller's sea lion and the elephant seals, this physical defense often results in bloody fighting and biting which sometimes bring death to the vanquished animal. In the colonies, the social standing of the bull depends upon the size of his territory and the number of cows he has claimed.

The time of year and length of the breeding season in the colonies depend a lot on the climate. In harsh environments, such as the Arctic and Antarctica, the season must be timed so that newborn seals (called *pups*) have the best chance of survival. Usually, pups are born in late winter or early spring.

Seal cows give birth on land to a single baby. At birth, the pups are covered with a soft, woolly fur that closely matches their environment in color; arctic and antarctic seals have a white fur at first, while those born in milder climates have darker coats. In time, the coats change color and become coarser.

Young seals grow at a very fast rate, especially in colder regions. Growth is much faster in proportion to their size than human babies or most land animals. The reason is that because of the harsh climate, which pinnipeds have chosen as a means of self-protection, pups must adjust to the world outside their colonies very quickly, and learn to swim and feed for themselves. Nature has provided that pups need only a short period of nursing their mothers before they are on their own. Some polar seals nurse only two or three weeks.

The milk of the cow seals is much different from that of whale cows. It contains much higher concentrations of fat and protein, which help account for the pups' very rapid growth.

Because most colonies are so remote from man, very little substantial information about seals and sea lions was collected by scientists until the past century. Even today, few details are known about the behavior and breeding habits of some of the thirty-one species.

Since the development of more reliable transportation and

diving equipment to observe the animals underwater, considerable more data is being compiled, however. As study continues, scientists are particularly interested in information about these animals that may help man himself as he explores the undersea world.

Seals and sea lions are marvelous divers. They can perform underwater feats and quickly attain depths that man finds impossible, even with modern diving equipment.

A gray seal once was accidentally caught on a fisherman's hook 500 feet down in the sea. Harp seals have been known to dive as deep as 825 feet, and two bladdernose seals exhibited at a zoo in Germany were caught in nets at depths of 1,200 and 1,260 feet. Because of the great hazards, human divers very seldom have gone deeper than 1,000 feet except in diving bells and submarines.

Seals and sea lions are capable of swimming as fast as twenty miles an hour in short bursts. And though they are air-breathing mammals like man, they can remain below for long periods without carrying an artificial air supply. Some remain below twenty minutes or so, but the Weddell seal, found in the Antarctic, has been timed as long as forty-three minutes, and is believed capable of dives even longer.

How do pinnipeds manage such feats? In recent experiments, scientists have found, for one thing, that seals have about one and a half times as much blood for their size as land mammals. Blood contains oxygen, which is what all mammals, including man, breathe. Scientists now theorize that when diving, there is a mechanism in the seal's system that shuts off the flow of oxygen going to the muscles and maintaining just enough oxygen to flow to vital organs such as the brain.

By doing so, this mechanism greatly reduces the heartbeat; underwater, a seal's heart may slow to only ten beats per minute as compared to 150 on the surface. Even under the great pres-

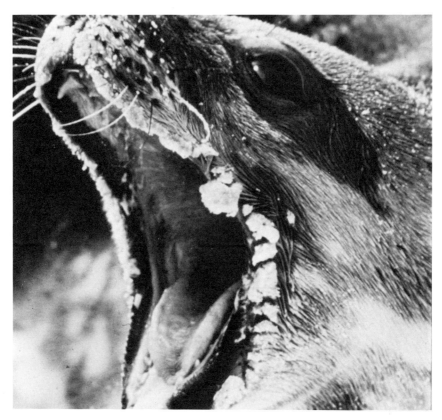

Weddell seals of the Antarctic are able to remain underwater for more than forty minutes at a time.

sure of the depths, the seal's body requires only a small amount of the energy needed at the surface. The diving seal also does not suffer from caisson disease, or "the bends," which has injured and killed many a human diver.

"The bends" occurs when nitrogen forms in the blood, due to pressure. Human divers must ascend slowly from the depths to allow this nitrogen to leave the system. Seals, however, take only a small amount of air with them as they dive, exhaling it as they go, so there is little nitrogen left to dissolve in the blood. As a result, they can surface very rapidly without "decompress-

21

ing" as human divers must.

Seals and sea lions are carnivorous. This means that their food consists of animals rather than plants. They eat fish and shellfish such as shrimp, krill, crayfish, or squid. Sometimes it is far below the surface that this food is found, and this is partly why seals must be able to reach the depths and remain there while they forage for their meals.

Pinnipeds that subsist mainly on fish have teeth more sharply pointed than those that eat invertebrates—small animals without backbones. In either case, though, seals have no broad molars that crush or grind food. Instead, they swallow their food whole, grinding it afterward in their stomachs. Most seals swallow stones to aid in this crushing process, just as chickens swallow gravel. (Some scientists believe that the stones also may help the seals maintain body balance when swimming.)

In varying degrees, the senses of sight and hearing help seals locate their food. It is known that seals have a developed sense of smell. Because the nostrils are closed underwater, however, this sense does them little good in that environment. (As an indication of how keen this sense is, it is by its individual odor that a mother can tell her own pup from others.)

The eyes of the seals and sea lions are large, much larger proportionately to their body than those of the other three groups of marine mammals. Seals that dive under the ice, where it is dark, have the largest eyes of all. A peculiarity of the eye is the lack of a tear duct. When on land, and when the seal's fur is dry, the seal looks as if it is constantly crying.

Although sight is useful to the seal in locating food, it is not the only sense aid. In various observations, scientists have found completely healthy, well-fed seals that were totally blind. So, hearing becomes another important food-finding sense.

Although seals' ears are small at the surface of the head, they are quite large and well developed internally. When the seal

22

Seals, such as this young elephant seal, are equipped with large eyes.

is submerged, the ear covering closes down tightly to prevent water from entering the head. Sound is conducted through water more audibly than through air, however, and underwater vibrations—those created by a swimming fish, for instance—are transmitted via the ear walls to the seal's brain, even though the ears are closed.

Recently, experiments by scientists indicate that seals' whiskers may assist in their hearing. One such research project was conducted by Dr. Thomas C. Poulter, an authority on animal sound and hearing systems, at Stanford University in California.

Because the seals' antenna-like whiskers are up to ten thousand times more sensitive than their ears, Dr. Poulter believes that they are very useful in transmitting vital information to the animal, such as the location and type of food. To test

23

UNIVERSITY SCHOOL LIBRARY
UNIVERSITY OF WYOMING

his theory, Dr. Poulter placed electrodes on nerves leading from the brain of an experimental seal to its whiskers. He then implanted another electrode in its inner ear for comparison. He found that while the ears did function, the whiskers were far more sensitive. He visualized them as a very delicate sonar system, sending out a series of small "clicks" which measured an object—food, for instance—and then bounced the information back to the whiskers and then the brain.

The system, Dr. Poulter believes, is infinitely more complicated than any sonar system built by man. Man's sonar is a device used mainly in ships and submarines to detect underwater objects by bouncing "clicks" off them.

Regardless of the kind of food it eats or how it finds it, the life of a young seal seems very harsh indeed. Many thousands die shortly after birth; less than half live to the age of three years. Some are victims of starvation, illness, storms, or are simply crushed to death under the weight of adult animals.

Others are killed by natural predators. These include the killer whale and shark that prey particularly on small, young seals that have entered the water to learn to swim. With one exception outside of the instinctive combat among males at breeding time, seals do not kill one another. The exception is the ferocious-looking leopard seal of the Antarctic which occasionally kills smaller species of seals, as well as penguins.

In nature, even this seemingly brutal ritual of killing and survival, or predator and prey, has a purpose. Except for man, who plants crops and raises domestic animals for food, no animal is able to regulate the availability of its food supply. To a large extent, the habitat of lower animals is selected on the basis of food supply.

If the populations of seals grew too large to be sustained by that food supply, starvation would result. As scientists explain, there is a balance in nature which keeps populations of all

24

organisms such as the pinnipeds fairly stable. On the other hand, there have been thousands of species of animals that were unable to survive the changes of evolution, and became extinct.

The seals and sea lions, which remind us so much of our fellow human beings in many ways, have thus far managed to survive. However, in the eighteenth century, man discovered that many of the pinnipeds were a valuable source of food and clothing, and that parts of their bodies could be converted into many other products. Widespread hunting resulted. And until laws were passed reducing and regulating the slaughter, some species of what one writer-naturalist called the "people of the sea" seemed destined to disappear from earth altogether.

3. Clowns of the Sea

Sea lions are often called the "clowns" of the sea. They are vocal, intelligent animals that train easily and do well in captivity.

Frequently, they are seen in sea circuses and marine ocean-arium shows, balancing balls on their noses, high-diving, and performing other tricks.

Because they live along the shoreline in temperate and sub-tropical waters, and because of their curiosity and keen intelligence, sea lions share a relatively close association with man, even in the wild. Yachtsmen often see them poking their heads curiously out of the water near their boats. Sometimes, sea lions follow boats for miles. This is especially true in the case of fishing boats from which the sea lions expect to retrieve scraps from cleaned fish that are thrown overboard. As with most pinnipeds, sea lions eat mostly fish, squid, and octopus.

Sea lions are playful animals and swift swimmers, spending many hours chasing each other in the sea. Sometimes they form long lines as they move, leaping out of the water like porpoises, tumbling and twirling their bodies before landing again. They also seem to enjoy riding the crests of waves as surfers do. Underwater, sea lions often swim near human divers, investigating them out of curiosity. They also seem to love to swim and

California sea lions performing at Sea World oceanarium.

Sea lion "porpoising" in water near Coronado Islands, Mexico.

Seals often float in the water with one of their flippers upraised.

float on their backs. While partly submerged in this position, an upraised flipper is occasionally mistaken for the fin of a shark.

The most familiar of these animals are the California sea lions. They are the most abundant and most commonly seen pinnipeds along the West Coast of the United States. This is their major range, although a few migrate north to Canada and south to the Baja California peninsula of Mexico.

California sea lions breed on offshore islands of North America. A second smaller group of about 20,000 animals populates the Galápagos Islands off South America. There is an even smaller population of only about 300 animals on Honshu Island in Japan. It has been many years since the latter animals have been seen, and some scientists think they may be extinct.

California sea lions are medium-sized animals, and are quite streamlined. They have big, round, soft eyes and fairly long

28

muzzles. Males grow to seven feet and weigh 600 pounds at maturity. Females are smaller, growing to six feet and 200 pounds. (In all species of pinnipeds except one—the leopard seal—mature males are larger and heavier than females.)

They vary in color, but generally are some shade of chocolate brown, with the top of the head becoming lighter with age.

Despite their popularity as "circus performers," their friendliness to man and the fact that their range is close to human populations, less is known about sea lions than some of the more remote species of pinnipeds. The Weddell seal of Antarctica, for instance, is far less accessible to scientists than the sea lions. Yet scientists have spent more time studying Weddell seals, mainly because of the animals' phenomenal diving ability. Information learned may prove valuable to human divers.

Recent research, however, has produced new information on the sea lions, especially about their breeding habits. Sea lion breeding rookeries are established on sandy, rocky, or boulder-strewn beaches. Sometimes these animals choose sea caves. After establishing harems of several females, males defend their territory by loud yelping and violent fighting. The breeding season for the California sea lion is June and July. Prior to this

California sea lion being rewarded for "sea circus" performance.

time, only the females inhabit the colonies, while the male bulls roam at sea.

Females give birth to a single young, usually between the middle of June and the middle of July. The pups are tended carefully by their mothers for only about two weeks. Then the young sea lions, gathering together, begin playing in shallow water and learning to swim, although they return to their mothers for about six months until they are weaned.

After the young are delivered and mating takes place for the following year's population, the males leave the rookeries. Often, they join colonies of other sea lions hundreds of miles distant. California sea lion males have been seen mingling with Steller's sea lions, a much larger species, as well as with still-larger elephant seals; in fact, they have been observed sleeping on top of these largest of all pinnipeds.

There are four other major species of sea lions, though none is as familiar as the California sea lion. Slightly larger and heavier is the southern sea lion, found on both the Pacific and Atlantic coasts of South America, and in the Falkland Islands. Mature males grow to eight feet and weigh 1,200 pounds; females reach six feet and 300 pounds. In common with all sea lions is the male's quite distinctive mustache and the agile swimming and diving ability of both sexes.

The southern sea lion also moves very swiftly on land. Scientists have found, however, that although these animals range far inland, they tire easily and often die before they are able to return to the sea.

The Australian sea lion is larger than either the California or southern species. Males reach twelve feet at maturity while females, only slightly smaller, grow to ten feet. As their name implies, they are found on the southern shores of Australia. There are believed to be only 2,000 to 10,000 of their species. They tend to congregate year-around in their colonies and do not migrate.

Steller sea lion, the largest of all sea lions.

Another pinniped native to Australia is the Hooker's sea lion. Numbering between 10,000 and 15,000 animals, they populate the Auckland Nature Reserve and Campbell Island, where the Australian government has protected them from hunters.

Largest of the sea lions is the Steller's sea lion, widely distributed in the North Pacific. It is also called the northern sea lion. Colonies of these massive animals (mature males weigh more than one ton) are found on both sides of the Pacific, in the islands of Japan as well as in the Pribilof Islands of Alaska. There are smaller colonies on coastal California islands.

Unlike the California sea lion, the Steller's sea lion seldom enters bays, estuaries, or river mouths. It prefers more remote colonies on rugged offshore islands. Prior to the twentieth century, there was a large breeding colony on Seal Rocks near San Francisco; scientists have also located skulls of pups on the Farallon Islands, twenty miles west of San Francisco. However, hunting and other man-made disturbances have reduced their colonies there to only a few animals, and have driven the main

Sea lion colony at Seal Rocks, near San Francisco, California.

populations away to more isolated locations.

The breeding colony social behavior of the Steller's sea lion resembles that of many other sea lion species, as well as that of the northern fur seal. Arriving at the colonies in early May, males establish their territory and choose their harems of many females. By late June or early July, after fierce battles between competing males have taken place, only the strongest bulls are left in the center of the colonies. Victorious bulls may each have as many as thirty females in their harems.

Defeated bulls are driven to the edge of the colonies, while younger males, not yet old enough to mate, often engage in mock battles of their own.

Steller's sea lion bulls carry scars of their battles throughout

32

their lives. Their powerful teeth and jaws can do considerable damage; the neck of the challenger seems to be a favorite target for the defender's attack.

Fighting is accompanied by loud roaring, a sound quite different from the doglike yelping of the California sea lion.

Pups are born during June and July. Their fur is a dark brownish gray that looks black when wet. At this age, they have not yet developed the roar of their fathers, and instead they bleat like young lambs. Scientists believe that this distinctive sound assists mothers in locating their young.

Shortly after birth, the pups begin to wander from their mothers, and many die during this difficult period of adjustment to life. Some are crushed to death by the carelessness of larger sea lions. Others perish on the reefs and rocks of their islands. Only instinct teaches them how to swim, which they learn to do in calmer tidepools of the islands. By the time they are about two months old, the pups spend much of their day exploring the surging channels of the islands and the open sea between them.

For years, many researchers wrote reports that Steller's sea lions could not be trained. They believed they were too large and too belligerent, and not as intelligent as the California sea lion. In 1972, however, a seven-foot long, 754-pound Steller's sea lion named Runner proved the scientists wrong. Runner was captured in 1969 by scientists of Stanford University as part of an interspecies interaction program with California sea lions. At that time, when he was four years old, he weighed about 625 pounds; even then, he was described by the scientists as "mean and untrainable."

Noting Runner's belligerence, the scientists donated him to the United States Navy's Bio-Science Facility at Point Mugu, California, where experiments with California sea lions and other marine mammals were taking place. Undaunted by Runner's antisocial behavior, an experienced animal trainer

"Runner," a Steller sea lion, being trained by Roland Raffler.

named Roland Raffler took charge. Raffler's patience, kindness, and sensitivity in handling Runner's early violent reactions overcame the animal's belligerence. Within a few days, Runner became accustomed to Raffler's gentle but firm attention. He let Raffler pet him. Gradually he began to cooperate. Later, he was participating easily and willingly in deep-diving tests in the open ocean.

"Steller's sea lions are really quite intelligent," Raffler recalled later. "Rather than follow a command or direction given in training, they stop to think through a command. They seem to try to figure out a way to do it or get out of doing it. They differ from California sea lions that are quite docile and more easily trained because they obediently follow directions."

34

Fishermen are seldom as pleased as Raffler with Steller's sea lions like Runner, however. Because the diet of these animals consists largely of fish, they often cause extensive damage to fishing nets from which they seek their meals. Salmon fishermen in the Pacific Northwest, particularly, have been forced to invest a lot of money in repairing and replacing nets. Many Steller's sea lions as well as other pinnipeds have been killed in the past because of this, although it is now illegal to kill or capture any marine mammal except by special permission.

Except for man, all sea lions have very few enemies. Occasionally they are killed by sharks or killer whales. Species in the Southern Hemisphere are occasionally preyed upon by the leopard seal. But far more perish at a young age in the breeding rookeries than fall prey to ocean predators later on in life.

For a long time, it was believed that the sea lion's habit of swallowing stones might be a cause of death. Found in the stomachs of dead animals, these stones range in size from walnuts to tennis balls. Later, it was theorized that sea lions use these stones to help digest food, in the way that chickens swallow sand and gravel to help digest their food. Still other scientists are trying to determine if perhaps these stones might also be a means of ballast, or balancing the body, while swimming underwater.

If sea lions survive the many hazards of their lives, they live a long time. A southern sea lion lived for 17½ years in the London Zoo, while a nineteen-year-old California sea lion established an even longer age record.

Once trained, sea lions, especially California sea lions, seem to have remarkable memories. Some have performed as long as ten years with only an occasional "refresher" training session required.

In recent years, man has attempted in many ways to help the sea lions whose activities both in the wild and as a captive

35

UNIVERSITY SCHOOL LIBRARY
UNIVERSITY OF WYOMING

Diese Dinge...

und noch viel mehr hat unser Wärter im Laufe von nur ein paar Wochen aus den Robbenbecken herausgesammelt

und so sah der geöffnete Magen unseres See-Elefanten ROLAND aus, der am 21.8.61 ein qualvolles Ende fand!

Liebe Zoobesucher! Helfen Sie mit unsere Tiere vor solchen Leiden zu bewahren!

A display at the Berlin (Germany) Zoo showing a number of man-made objects which were found in the stomach of a single dead seal.

performer have given him pleasure. As one example, the Sea World oceanarium in San Diego, California, regularly "adopts" young California sea lions that have been found stranded on nearby beaches.

Some are sick. Others are lost. Many are yearlings that have been pushed out of their colonies by their mothers who are ready to give birth to a new generation. Although this may seem cruel, it is nature's way, a fact of life in the world of the pinnipeds.

In the spring, Sea World receives as many as three or four sea lions picked up on local beaches each week by the Humane Society. At Sea World, teams of experts provide medical attention and food. Each new arrival is given a thorough examination, vitamins, and antibiotics. They are then kept in a quarantine area and watched closely for symptoms of pneumonia or other distress.

Sea lions normally will not eat vitamin tablets. To overcome this, the pills are crushed into powder and inserted into fish which are in turn fed to the animals.

Some of the sea lions respond to this care and become permanent residents of the oceanarium. They are either trained for shows or placed on exhibit at a seal feeding pool. From time to time, sick or injured young Steller's sea lions are also cared for at Sea World, and entertain visitors by frolicking with their California sea lion relatives.

Many of the "orphans" are returned to the sea if scientists feel that even after being pampered by man they will be able to compete in the wild.

Rehabilitation programs such as that at Sea World go a long way toward helping sick or injured pinnipeds that have left their own environment and joined man's. It was only recently, however, that man took steps to assist in the survival of seals and sea lions in the sea itself.

By expanding their research, scientists are learning more about the factors that affect pinniped survival in the wild. They have learned, for instance, that human visitors to rookeries at the time of year seals are giving birth can cause disturbed parent animals to accidentally crush their young. Based on this knowledge, those who want to observe seals in their habitat are encouraged to do so at other times of the year.

Just as importantly, governments have at last placed controls on the kind of indiscriminate hunting of seal populations that for most of a century seemed destined to drive some species to extinction altogether.

4. The Fur Seals

In the primeval loneliness of the Pribilof Islands of Alaska, the presence of vast colonies of northern fur seals is one of the most spectacular sights and sounds in nature.

Their loud coughs, barks, and bleats echo over a great distance. Near the edge of the barren, rocky islands, the sounds mingle with the hiss of the surf, and manage to be heard even over the roar of arctic wind.

During the summer breeding season, before the seals begin their long southward migration to escape winter weather, the Pribilofs teem with bodies that wriggle as if a single mass. There is a drama of life in the Pribilofs. There is also death. Each year, more than half of the estimated 500,000 pups born die from various causes within days of their birth. The major killers: infections from hookworms and other diseases. Because of the seals' social nature of crowding together, some are trampled to death; others die from starvation, even though young seals normally learn to find their own food shortly after birth.

For millennia, however, until man arrived in the Pribilofs, the northern fur seal managed to survive these many hazards. Its population once could be counted in the millions. Even today, the main colony on St. George and St. Paul islands numbers more than 1.5 million animals. In terms of total individuals, this

An old print showing a seal rookery on the Pribilof Islands.

makes the colony the largest aggregation of mammals in one place anywhere on earth, larger than the great caribou herds of North America, vaster than any of the remaining herds of African game.

At the height of the period of uncontrolled hunting of the northern fur seal, its total population plunged to below 200,000. True, that is still a lot of animals, far more than what scientists consider a danger level in the decline toward extinction. Yet had that hunting continued unchecked, it seems certain that this species probably would have disappeared from earth.

Still the center of great controversy, the exploitation by man of the northern (or Alaskan) fur seal has brought about perhaps the most extensive study of any of the pinnipeds, with the possible exception of Antarctica's Weddell seal.

The northern fur seal is one of nine species of fur seals which collectively represent more than one-fourth of all pinniped species. As seals go, it is a fairly small animal. Males attain a length of about seven feet at maturity, and weigh 600 pounds. Adult females weigh 300 pounds and are about five feet long.

As their name suggests, they are covered with a dark, rich brown fur, or hair. On most animals, white hairs intermingle

A northern fur seal mother (right) and pup.

with the dark ones at the neck; females are generally lighter in color than the males. When the pups are born, they are covered with a coarse black hair which is shed at eight weeks and replaced by a coat of steel gray that later matures to rich brown.

The annual cycle of life in the arctic fur seal colonies begins in June when the males return from their southern migration to establish territories they will guard—by roaring and fighting—during the breeding season. A few weeks later, the females arrive. The birth of the pups occurs between June 20 and July 20.

The mother seal remains with her pup for only about a week. Then she leaves to seek food in the sea, returning about once a week to suckle her young. Although fur seal pups can swim at birth, it is usually about a month before they venture into the water. Meanwhile, the young gather in great groups or pods, dividing their day between playing and sleeping.

As winter nears, the great arctic colonies are suddenly emptied once again. In terms of both herd size and distance traveled, one

A young northern fur seal feeding.

of the greatest migrations in the world of nature then begins. During winter and spring, herds of tens of thousands of animals swim south, a few toward Japan but most of them along the western coast of North America. In past years, a few Alaskan fur seals have been sighted in the winter as far south as San Diego, thousands of miles from their summer homes in the Pribilofs.

Due largely to the time they spend each year in migrating, fur seals probably spend a greater portion of their lives in the water than other species of pinnipeds. Scientists studying them have learned that they seek their food in the sea in the evening, devoting the daytime to sleeping and playing on land. Fur seals can dive to about 240 feet and subsist mostly on herring and squid.

The islands of the Pribilofs are named for Gerasim Pribilof, an eighteenth-century Russian navigator, explorer, and fur trader. He visited them during an expedition in 1786–87. At that time, the fur seal population numbered an estimated 2.5

41

UNIVERSITY SCHOOL LIBRARY
UNIVERSITY OF WYOMING

million animals. The credit for discovery of the seals, though, belongs to Georg Wilhelm Steller, who accompanied Vitus Bering on a search for Alaska in 1741. On August 10 of that year, Steller sighted what he believed to be fur seals. The following summer he returned to Bering Island where he was shipwrecked. While awaiting rescue, he made many close studies of the seals and later published the first full account of their biology and behavior.

While the account proved of tremendous value to scientists, it also attracted the interest of hundreds of fur traders from around the world. Along with the harp seal, another heavily hunted species, the northern fur seal soon became the most valuable pinniped in the world in terms of commercial value.

Before Bering, Steller, and other Europeans arrived, fur seals were hunted and killed only by native Eskimos. To the Eskimo, a seal was not an object of commercial exploitation. It was necessity that required the killing of these animals.

The Eskimos used the seals for clothing, food, and tools.

From the fur, clothing could be made to ward off the subzero cold of winter. Knives and other tools were fashioned from the bones. From the skin and other parts of the seal's body came the necessary raw materials to make boots, hulls of boats, oil for lamps, and harpoon lines. The seal's meat became a staple of the Eskimo diet.

Although the voyages by Europeans to the Arctic for purely commercial gain began in the eighteenth century, it was in the mid-nineteenth century that sealing—or seal hunting—reached its peak. At one time, hunters killed about 300,000 seals each year. Although it is illegal under international law today, many of them were hunted in the water. Often, seals were merely wounded and sank in the sea before the hunters could retrieve them. This was particularly tragic when the hunted seal was a pregnant mother about to give birth.

By 1867, when the United States acquired Alaska from Russia, the fur seal population was at its lowest point. Only about 200,000 animals remained out of 2.5 million. Since then, many nations have joined in agreements to regulate seal hunting in the Pribilofs, as well as among the harp seals in the Arctic of eastern Canada.

The first such agreement, the Fur Seals Treaty, was signed in 1911 by the United States, Great Britain (including Canada), Japan, and Russia. Its main condition was to prohibit pelagic sealing, the killing of seals in the water. Based on studies of biologists who watched the animals closely, later agreements also established "quotas" or limits on the number of seals that can be hunted each year.

Today, about 60,000 to 70,000 northern fur seals are killed by hunters each year. Commercial hunters call this "harvesting." The season starts about June 20, after the seals have returned to the Pribilofs from their summer wanderings, and lasts from a month to five weeks.

Arriving in boats, native hunters trained on the seal islands drive the animals inland where they can be herded more easily. After the seals have been killed, their carcasses are sent to processing plants where they are converted into pet food, oil, soap, and other products.

Although seal fur is still used to make coats in many countries, it is now illegal in the United States to sell any product made from a marine mammal.

Harp seals have also been widely hunted. Although they are not classed scientifically among the true fur seals, they are covered with a furlike hair highly prized by hunters. They are also sought for the oil their bodies produce. About half the profits from harp seals comes from the oil of older animals, while among the young, it is the hair that is most valuable.

Harp seals are hunted mostly on islands and ice floes of eastern Canada during the summer. It is here that these animals form their breeding rookeries, in March. An estimated 100,000 to 200,000 new harp seals are born each year in these colonies.

Under pressure from humane societies and other groups, the Canadian and Norwegian governments changed the harp sealing laws in 1970. It is now illegal to hunt these seals from aircraft, and the hunting season itself has been delayed until late March and early April to give the pups time to shed their white birthcoats, to be weaned, and to learn to swim.

Altogether, the hunting of fur seals in North America amounts to an estimated $8 million industry each year, and it remains the center of controversy.

Certainly, there are two sides to the question of whether seals should be killed for commercial gain. Many conservationists argue that the killing should be halted altogether. Killing seals, they say, is immoral, and the methods used are inhumane. They say that many of the products derived from seals can now be made from nonanimal substances.

44

The hunters contend, on the other hand, that because of legal limits on the number of animals killed each year, the total population of any species is not likely to fall below that necessary to reproduce and survive. Further, they suggest, controlled hunting actually helps to maintain a balance between seals and their food supply. Without "thinning" the colonies each year, they argue, seals might overpopulate and some would starve because the food supply would not be adequate for all.

If nothing else, the controversy has served to focus worldwide attention on these seals. This applies also to their arctic breeding grounds. Noted biologist Victor B. Scheffer has proposed that the Pribilofs be designated a great international park of education and wildlife study. Hunting would be prohibited. Dr. Scheffer spent more than thirty years of his life with the United States Fish and Wildlife Service, many of them living in the lonely Pribilofs, observing, photographing, and writing about the herds of fur seals there.

He notes that these islands, once closed to outside visitors except by special permission, have become a popular attraction for "amateur naturalists" carrying not guns or clubs, but cameras.

Explaining his proposal to encourage more of this, he wrote: "The seals would suddenly appear in the spring, glistening wet in the May sun, and after their summer ashore, disappear into the sea fogs of November. They would give birth and mate, some would fight to the death, and pups would be trampled in the mire of the rookeries. As in any national park, the whole splendid cycle of life, death, and regeneration would be played continuously before the eyes of visitors."

There would have to be safeguards under such a plan, so that the animals would not be molested or unduly frightened by the human visitors. An incident that occurred on San Miguel Island, off the coast of Southern California, would seem to prove that seals thrive best when man's impact is minimized.

45

UNIVERSITY SCHOOL LIBRARY
UNIVERSITY OF WYOMING

In the middle of the nineteenth century, before Southern California was heavily populated, a large northern fur seal colony thrived on San Miguel. As humans began to visit the island, the seal population began to decline. Soon, there were no seals left at all.

Then the island was placed under the jurisdiction of the United States Navy and closed to outside visitors. Nearly a century later, in 1967, a surprising discovery was made. In small numbers, the fur seals had begun to return to San Miguel. At that time, a visiting biologist counted about 100 animals.

Five years later, under continuing protection, the population had increased to an estimated 600, and it is still growing. Living on rocky beaches, they share the solitude of their island home with colonies of elephant seals, sea otters, California sea lions, and thousands of seabirds.

A second example is the story of the Guadalupe fur seal. A fairly small seal (males reach six feet; females are considerably smaller) this species was once widely distributed all along the West Coast of North America. But it, too, became a victim of hunters in large numbers.

Between 1810 and 1812, records show, 73,402 skins of fur seals were taken from the Farallon Islands off San Francisco alone. The records did not distinguish between pelts of northern fur seals and Guadalupe fur seals. But since hunting occurred at a time of year when northern fur seals normally were absent from the island, it was assumed that most of the animals were of the Guadalupe species.

Unlike many seals that live on beaches or flat, rocky coastlines, Guadalupe fur seals spend much of their lives in sea caves. Despite this apparent protection, hunting greatly decimated their population in the nineteenth century. Some scientists, in fact, thought the species had become extinct.

In the 1950s, however, a small colony numbering only a few

New Zealand fur seal.

hundred animals was discovered on Guadalupe Island, off the West Coast of Mexico. There, isolated from human impact, the same cycle of "life, death, and regeneration" that Dr. Scheffer described, goes on year after year.

Hopefully, the Guadalupe fur seal's population will continue to increase, and not fall below the level where extinction will follow. In that way, one more species of man's fellow mammals will be around for a long time to enrich man's own being.

5. How Seals Adapt

To the casual observer, the ice-locked polar continent of Antarctica seems a forbidding place, devoid of life. Actually, the reverse is true. To the human visitor, not adapted to life there, Antarctica is indeed inhospitable. Winds of 200 miles an hour are not unusual. To fall into the icy ocean means almost instant death.

Yet this vast region of earth, covered with ice and snow the year around, supports an amazing variety of animal life, including several species of pinnipeds. The reason is the rich abundance of organisms in the water that provide a constant food source for animals large and small, including seals.

Through research, scientists have learned that the waters of Antarctica are in fact richer in living organisms than many areas of the warm tropical ocean, which were once believed to be the most abundant on earth.

The rich supply of tiny plant food, called phytoplankton, is eaten by tiny animals (zooplankton) that are in turn devoured by seals, whales, birds, and large fishes. There are an estimated one hundred species of fish around and under the antarctic ice alone, and some are very large. It is the low temperature of the water that permits the Antarctic Ocean to provide in heavy abundance the dissolved nutrients and salts necessary for the extensive plankton growth.

To survive Antarctica's bitter cold, seals living there have necessarily become highly adapted through evolution. Not only has nature given them special protection such as extra thick body-warming blubber, but they have acquired specialized physical features to assist them in feeding and moving about in this wintry wilderness. For these reasons, they have become fascinating subjects for scientific investigation.

The Weddell seal, for example, has developed two special features for antarctic survival. The first is a highly developed set of teeth with which it can saw holes in the ice and then spend a part of the winter underneath where it is warmer. The second is an ability to dive extremely deep to find food that would otherwise be unobtainable.

Weddell seals can dive as deep as 1,800 feet and remain

The Weddell seal is well adapted for its life in the Antarctic.

A Weddell seal pup.

submerged up to forty minutes; they have brought fish up from those depths that would otherwise be unknown to man.

A large, tubby animal, the Weddell seal weighs up to 900 pounds at maturity and lives closer to the South Pole than any other pinniped. Its population now numbers about 500,000, possibly escaping widespread slaughter by hunters due to its geographical isolation.

Migrating very little, the Weddell seal's reproduction season is from September to January. This is a period of warm weather in the Southern Hemisphere where the seasons are reversed. Leaving the sea, the females arrive first at the rookeries established on ice floes and pack ice, and deliver their single young a few days later. Then the males join them to mate for the following year.

Weddell seals are among the most protective of the pinnipeds as mothers. They fiercely defend their newborn young, barking and snapping at any intruder. So strong is this instinct that some have been observed remaining with their pups long after the young have died.

The mother seal does not eat during the six weeks she nurses her young. The pups, only about 4½ feet long at birth, and weighing sixty pounds, are covered with a thick rusty-gray coat with no markings. They grow rapidly, however; by the time they are weaned, they have gained 300 pounds or more and are then ready to begin the task of hunting their own food.

As with most seals, the mortality rate of Weddell seals is very high. As many as half of them die in some colonies before they are weaned, many of them accidentally crushed by other seals or by shifting pack ice.

Their food consists of squid, cuttlefish, shrimp, and fish. Sometimes mud, sand, and stones are swallowed with the food. Scientists believe these may help in digestion.

When the temperature begins to drop, indicating the approach of winter, Weddell seals begin their move to below the ice where it is much warmer. They do this by chewing holes in the ice with their teeth, and then breathing in small natural air pockets on the underside of the floe. If the air supply in these "domes" is insufficient, they enlarge the opening with their teeth.

Under the ice, Weddell seals travel about freely during the winter, and they have been heard calling to one another as if relaying information on where food is available.

When the antarctic spring arrives and the ice begins to break up, the Weddells emerge from their under-ice winter homes and move away. They do not venture very far, however, and because they travel about so awkwardly on the ice, they spend a great deal of their lives in the water.

In their extensive study of this species of pinnipeds, scientists

51

UNIVERSITY SCHOOL LIBRARY
UNIVERSITY OF WYOMING

A close-up look at the crab-eater seal's teeth.

have observed what they call a strong "instinct of retirement." This refers to the habit of sick, injured, or dying seals moving away from the main herd. Some Weddell seal bodies have been found in glaciers 3,000 feet above sea level. This instinctive drive is common among many other pinnipeds.

To the crabeater seal, another antarctic species, nature has provided an unusual set of teeth which function as a "strainer" to take in small crustaceans called *krill*—its only food. Krill are tiny, reddish, shrimplike animals that travel about in vast swarms near the ocean surface in antarctic waters. They are also the chief diet of the baleen whales.

After ingesting a mouthful of krill, the crabeater then partially closes its mouth, clamping the "strainer" down. Water taken in with the krill is then drained out, while the filter retains the food for swallowing.

Crabeater seals, which grow to about nine feet in length and weigh 500 pounds, are probably the most abundant pinnipeds in the world. There are an estimated 2 million to 5 million of them altogether along the shoreline of the antarctic continent. A few have been seen in Australia and New Zealand.

A third example of adaptation is the leopard seal. The only pinniped known to prey regularly on other seals and sea lions, it, too, is a resident of the pack ice of Antarctica, as well as islands of South America, New Zealand, and Australia.

The leopard seal's ferocious nature, many scientists suggest, may account for its solitary habits, which are unusual among the socially active pinnipeds. It is one of the few pinnipeds, perhaps the only one, that doesn't travel in herds. Rarely have more than two leopard seals been sighted together.

Because so little is known about this species, accurate information is not available on whether this is also the case during the breeding and reproductive seasons, the time of year when most pinnipeds gather in their huge colonies.

A crabeater seal on the ice.

Two leopard seals.

As "loners" of the pinniped world, leopard seals use their ferocious nature to their advantage; because they are better able to defend themselves against predators, they may not feel the protective need of colonizing.

Although fish and cephalopods are a major part of their diet, the leopard seals feed on penguins and pups of other seal species. Sometimes they will scavenge on the carcass of large marine mammals such as whales. Occasionally, they even eat sea plants.

Their fast swimming ability is another means of adaptive protection. Unlike many seals that seem clumsy as they climb onto land or ice floes, leopard seals can move from water to land very swiftly. As a result of both speed and ferociousness, perhaps, the leopard seal's only known predator is the killer whale.

Because they comprise one entire suborder of the order

Carnivora, or flesh-eaters, many general statements can be made about all pinnipeds. But in their continuing research, scientists have learned that there are exceptions to the many general rules of their biology, behavior, and reproduction, and these are due largely to environmental adaptation.

While most seals are gregarious, traveling in groups, the leopard seal does not, as we have seen. The crabeater is the only seal known to possess the unique strainer-like set of teeth. And although we classify seals and sea lions as "true marine mammals"—meaning that they live entirely in salt water—one species is an exception to this rule, too.

It is the Baikal seal, the only pinniped that lives its life entirely in fresh water. There are about 40,000 to 100,000 of these unusual, small seals, which rarely exceed 4½ feet in length or weigh more than 150 pounds.

They are named for Lake Baikal in Siberia of the Soviet Union, the deepest freshwater lake in the world, where their entire population lives. It is still a mystery to science how or why these animals originally came to a body of water nearly 1,500 miles from the nearest salt water. Nor is much known about their summer activities, since they spend these months in areas of the giant lake inaccessible to human visitors.

The winter life style of the Baikal seal, however, has long been studied. Once again, it illustrates how animals through evolution have become adapted to a particular environment and how they have acquired special features to adjust to that environment.

During the Russian winter, Lake Baikal freezes over and the temperature remains far below zero degrees. Although the water of the lake is fresh, the winter there is much like that of Antarctica.

When the lake begins to freeze in late fall, the Baikal seal, like the Weddell seal, chews holes to gain access to the water

55

UNIVERSITY SCHOOL LIBRARY
UNIVERSITY OF WYOMING

below the ice where the temperature is much higher than that of the air above. Emerging through holes in the ice, pregnant females then construct dens out of snow that has piled on top. To accomplish this, they burrow into the snow and wiggle around until their body heat has thawed out a snow den usually about three feet in diameter. The sides of the den serve to protect the pups that will be born there later from severe winds that sweep the 400-mile long, mile-deep lake. After building the dens, the females join the males under the ice, breathing air trapped in pockets like the Weddell seals.

Pups, born in mid-March, are tiny creatures; they weigh but eight pounds and measure only two feet long. They remain in their dens for many weeks. Only when the ice is completely melted and it is safe to do so, do they venture into the water to learn to swim.

Though not a cold-water pinniped, the common or harbor seal is more proof that statements about pinnipeds do not necessarily apply to all species. Most seals give birth on land. The pups of harbor seals, however, are born in the water, just like the babies of whales and porpoises.

The reproduction season is from May to October. This is the time when pregnant females congregate in bays in great numbers. The two-foot long babies, weighing up to twenty-five pounds, are very weak at first, and cannot swim. They are very buoyant, however, and they drift to the surface where they gulp their first breath of air.

Mother harbor seals nurse their young underwater and do not leave the pups' side until they have learned to swim. Then the young must face life entirely alone.

Harbor seals are found on the coasts of most continents. Males grow to about six feet in length and weigh 550 pounds; females are about half that size and length. As their name implies, they frequently visit harbors, bays, and estuaries, leaving the water

A harbor seal in the Berlin Zoo.

to spend part of their lives on sand flats or mud banks.

Probably because of its close contact with man, the harbor seal is a cautious animal and instinct has taught it to be wary of humans. Some scientists believe that this instinct of survival is so strong that harbor seals have learned to tell whether boats near them have humans aboard or are empty.

As pinnipeds go, harbor seals are fairly fast swimmers, traveling up to fifteen miles an hour in short bursts by "sculling" with their flippers. Unlike most seals, they do not dive rapidly, however. They sink slowly, like submarines, and can remain submerged up to forty-five minutes. They cannot sleep in the water like some seals, but must haul themselves onto beaches or mud banks to do so.

6. The Elephant Seals

True giants of the sea, the elephant seals are the largest and heaviest of the pinnipeds. At maturity, males reach a length of over twenty feet and weigh an estimated 8,000 pounds, or four tons. Females are considerably smaller than males, but as pinnipeds go, they are still imposing animals. They grow to over five feet and weigh up to 2,000 pounds.

Elephant seals derive their name from the male's bulbous, inflatable, trunklike proboscis, or nose. The elephant seal can send out a wide range of grunts and roars by inflating its proboscis. At mating time, the island rookeries of the animal are very noisy places as a result.

There are two closely related species of elephant seals today. The southern elephant seal inhabits the Southern Hemisphere and is found on islands around the Antarctic. The northern elephant seal, distributed many thousands of miles distant, is found on islands off the West Coast of Mexico north to central California.

During the heyday of seal hunting, the elephant seal, like the Guadalupe fur seal, was headed toward certain extinction. Because of their great size and considerable blubber, thousands were killed each year for oil and hides. Because the blubber of a single mature male seal could yield up to 150 gallons of oil,

Close-up of the head of a male elephant seal, showing proboscis.

these animals were very profitable commercially.

It was the elephant seal's gentle nature that helped account for its near-extinction. In the wild, the northern species has few natural enemies and no fear of man. It was simple for sealers to walk up to them and shoot them in the head. The seal would be skinned and the blubber separated from the body on the spot. In some areas of hunting, elephant seals were herded into fenced corrals like domestic cattle for easier slaughtering.

For about fifty years, the hunting continued. Once-crowded rookeries along the West Coast were nearly empty. Finally, in 1911, the Mexican government placed the seals under partial protection and later made it permanent. In 1957, the California Department of Fish and Game, responsible for the welfare of

59

UNIVERSITY SCHOOL LIBRARY
UNIVERSITY OF WYOMING

pinnipeds in that state, made it illegal to hunt elephant seals.

Granted protection, the animal's population began to increase and today it is plentiful once again. The largest single colony, of 15,000 seals, is on Guadalupe Island, off the western coast of Baja California. In 1960, a breeding colony was established on Año Nuevo Island, near San Francisco, and young have been born there every year since.

Because Año Nuevo can be reached easily from the California mainland, it is an ideal place for scientists to study the elephant seal. Considerable research has been done by Dr. Burney J. LeBeouf, of the University of California.

As with most pinnipeds, Dr. LeBeouf found, during long periods of observation at Año Nuevo, that elephant seals are very social animals. But because of their great size and weight, the fighting among bull animals in defending their territory and harems is among the bloodiest of the pinnipeds.

To the male elephant seal, the timing of the arrival at a rookery is critical. Too early, he may have to fight too long and become exhausted by the time the females are ready for mating. Too late, and the choicer harems may have already been selected by other bulls.

His timing, therefore, accounts largely for his success in the social hierarchy of the breeding rookery. Defending the ground he has claimed, the bull first attempts to frighten away his challengers by trumpeting a series of low-pitched grunts through his proboscis. If this does not work, the sound is increased in pitch. If the challenger persists, the battle begins.

The bull rears back and lunges at his foe with the upper part of his body. Equipped with large, strong teeth, a mature elephant seal can deliver a very effective and painful bite.

Some of these battles last nearly an hour. Before victory is decided, the water around the rookery flows red with the blood of the loser. Once the quarrel is over, however, there is great

An elephant seal trumpeting.

respect within the colony for the victor. Vanquished bulls
usually leave the colony until the following year. Those losing
their battles on Año Nuevo, Dr. LeBeouf found, usually swam
to the California mainland several miles away, and remained
there during the balance of the breeding season.

In some colonies, bulls have been known to retain their
number one position in the rookery hierarchy for several years.
They are known as the Alpha bulls. And by mating with many
female seals each year, Dr. LeBeouf suggests, "a bull will father
many offspring and his attributes, such as sturdy canine teeth,
thick neck shield, and great size, will be perpetuated."

Bulls do not eat during the ninety-day mating season, and
they sleep only when other seals are sleeping. Thus it is that
only by keen vigilance and brute strength do the top-ranking

61

bulls manage to maintain their social status year after year.

Below the level of the bulls at the top of the social structure, however, the mortality rate is considerably higher. Dr. LeBeouf found at Año Nuevo that thirty of the thirty-five bulls born in 1965 died before they reached maturity eight years later. The main predators are large sharks, killer whales, and man. Among southern elephant seals, leopard seals are also predators.

After giving birth to their single pup, female elephant seals of both northern and southern species regularly go to the water, possibly to feed. They are excellent swimmers and divers, reportedly attaining depths of 2,000 feet where they can remain up to ten minutes. Their diet consists mainly of fish, cuttlefish, and cephalapods.

Bull (left) and cow elephant seal.

An elephant seal pup.

The young nurse for three to four weeks and their weight quadruples during this time. After about a month, the females leave the rookeries.

The males ignore the babies almost entirely. In moving about, in fact, they often unintentionally crush the pups to death under their enormous weight.

Females can become quite aggressive toward intruders during the breeding season. Although they do not have the large bladder-like nose of the males, they do grunt and bark to warn any other animals or humans away.

During the rest of the year, animals of both sexes are very gentle, and pay little attention to people. Scientists often have reported being able to walk freely among them, even sitting on them occasionally.

During the making of a movie about elephant seals, Jacques-Yves Cousteau, the French oceanographer, made an interesting discovery regarding this. The animals were at first nervous as

An elephant seal undergoing training at Sea World oceanarium.

Cousteau's crewmen walked among them, but they relaxed and paid no attention when the humans crouched on their hands and knees and crawled. Cousteau theorized that while the standing men suggested danger to the seals, crouching ones did not.

Baby elephant seals are black bundles of curly fur and flippers, weighing 65 to 75 pounds at birth. When they are a month old, ignored by their fathers and abandoned by their mothers, they begin the solitary, roving phase of their life cycle. They are completely on their own.

For the males, life may last as long as twenty-four years. The life span of females is about half as long. The chance of either to live this long is considerably better today, due to man's protection. The major obstacles now are only those that nature has provided.

64

7. Seals, Sea Lions, and Man

As air-breathing mammals that are born live and have biological systems similar to those of humans, seals and sea lions have long interested scientists.

Humans possess an intelligence much higher than that of the pinnipeds. Yet, in some ways, especially in the sea, seals and sea lions are superior to man. They can dive more rapidly, remain below for long periods without artificial breathing devices, and swim faster.

The oceans cover more than two-thirds of the earth's surface. It is in their depths that all life on earth began. The oceans are what make the earth unique among the planets. Without them, neither humans nor seals and sea lions could exist.

Only recently in man's history has he begun to seriously explore and study the depths of the life-giving seas. In many ways they are important in fulfilling man's needs; they are a vast source of food, energy, fuel, medicine, and even fresh water.

Before the invention of portable air supply devices which divers can carry along on their underseas journeys, both depth and length of descent were quite limited. Even with such equipment, humans are not nearly as capable underwater as the seals, sea lions, and other marine mammals. By studying how the pinnipeds adapt so well to the underwater world, scientists are seeking means by which they can help humans in underwater exploration and scientific discovery.

The body system that allows seals to dive quickly, for instance, is being studied in relationship to lung diseases in humans. One such project was undertaken by the University of California at San Diego, using seals and sea lions of Scripps Institution of Oceanography. Later, dolphins were added to the project.

The "star" of the medical research was a California sea lion named Houdini, who learned to do tricks that could help the researchers, like blowing air from his lungs into a gas collector following a dive.

By studying the exhaled air, researchers hoped to better understand the intricate mechanism by which the animal could avoid the "bends" and other diving hazards faced by humans. In turn, this information may help medical science in finding ways to prevent or treat lung diseases such as chronic bronchitis and emphysema.

Later, the researchers plan to add Weddell seals to the sea lions, because of their even-greater diving ability.

The possibility of seals and sea lions helping humans was first suggested by a project called "Quick Find," begun in 1969 by the United States Navy. Sponsored by the Naval Undersea Center (NUC) in San Diego, California, researchers taught trained California sea lions to dive to 500 feet and attach "grabber" devices to submerged objects for recovery.

Before Quick Find, recovery of objects such as torpedoes and missiles was done by human divers, expensive grappling equipment—or not at all. While humans now can dive to depths of 1,000 feet or more, doing so is both expensive and risky. Two sea lions named Turk and Fatman proved, however, that man's mammal friends in the sea can be quite useful as an alternate means of deep-water recovery.

The harnessed sea lion is easily led by handler, Jim Corey. This method of animal movement greatly reduces transportation difficulties.

NUC scientists first selected a number of sea lions from colonies off the California coast, and flew them to Hawaii where they were placed in training.

"Sea lions adapt quickly to a training environment," Martin E. Conboy, project leader, explained later. "They can be captured wild, and within two or three weeks, will submit to a harness." Using a harness, a trainer can lead a sea lion about like a dog. If it is a very long leash, the trainer can maintain control during training in the open ocean.

Although porpoises and killer whales were used in later experiments, and though they can dive deeper than pinnipeds, NUC researchers found that seals and sea lions enjoy one major advantage over the cetaceans: because they can comfortably remain far longer out of water, they can be transported and cared for more easily.

Conboy remembers of the project: "Sea lions are small. They're easy to transport and thus conceivably can be moved about quickly anywhere in the world. And they're intelligent enough to adapt to training rapidly and perform well underwater. To us, they proved to be a very effective recovery system."

Quick Find consists of two or three men, a rubber boat, a reel of nylon line, a pinger receiver, a grabber device—and one cooperative sea lion.

The animal is taught to locate an underwater object, such as a rocket, by "homing in" on an acoustic pinger attached to the object. Later, as it becomes more proficient, it learns to locate its target entirely by eyesight.

During early training, the animal is "worked" in shallow water, starting about a hundred yards from the submerged target. While one trainer operates the rubber boat, another tends the sea lion. A third places the boat in position over the object, locating it by listening to its pinger through earphones. The sea lion is then released; it reports that it has heard the pinger by returning to the surface and pressing a rubber disc in the boat with its nose.

At that point, a "grabber" device shaped like a crescent moon, is strapped to the sea lion's head. It holds a nylon line strong enough to lift a 2,000-pound object. As the animal dives to the missile or other target, the line unreels. When the sea lion presses the grabber against the target, it clamps itself on and releases itself from the sea lion's head. Trainers in the boat can then reel in the underwater object.

The first major test of Quick Find, in 1970, involved Turk and Fatman, two California sea lions that had been trained in Hawaii. Turk was trained to perform the recovery; Fatman was a "backup animal," to be used if for some reason Turk did not perform as expected.

The sea lion is trained to climb on the harnessing stand. In this position the trainer can conveniently harness the animal. Harnessing the animals prior to work in the open sea are Jim Corey with "Fatman" (left) and Chief Gordon Sybrant with "Turk" (right).

The grabber device, easily manipulated by the animal, fits snuggly over the animal's snout. When this device is pressed against the underwater target by the sea lion, the grabber encircles it and locks on.

UNIVERSITY SCHOOL LIBRARY
UNIVERSITY OF WYOMING

The sea lion, Turk, attaches the grabber device to a target during a training session at the Naval Undersea Center's Hawaii Laboratory at Kaneohoe. The target can now be raised to the surface by the recovery team above the water. Sea lions have made successful recoveries at depths of 500 feet.

Specifically, NUC researchers wanted to know if the two animals would be adversely affected by a long, 2,500-mile flight from Hawaii to the California coast where a rocket was to be recovered after being fired from Hawaii.

Happily for the NUC team, the two animals were not disturbed by the long flight. Although dense fog set in at the project site, Turk located the rocket as scheduled, attached the grabber, and swam quickly back to the surface. For the first time in Navy history, a mammal other than man had been used to locate and attach recovery equipment to an operational test device.

So successful were the Quick Find experiments that NUC in 1972 turned the program over to another Navy unit, at Coronado, California, for further testing. Trainers at Coronado hope to extend not only the depth at which sea lions can work, but the variety of objects to be recovered.

During these various tests, the Navy trainers learned that unlike many trained animals, seals and sea lions often will perform even if they are not rewarded by food. The willingness to do so depends a lot on the individual animal. Some refuse to work at all unless rewarded every time. Fatman, however, once made 146 dives in succession, in water fifty to sixty feet deep, working long after his handlers had run out of fish. Many marine scientists attribute this to the pinnipeds' high level of intelligence. Some now believe that this intelligence ranks with that of the porpoise, once considered the "brainiest" mammal in the sea. The porpoise is another animal which often performs solely for the joy of it, and not necessarily for a reward.

Ultimately, the Navy researchers believe, sea lions like Turk and Fatman may perform a wide variety of underwater tasks, such as locating and helping to recover sunken submarines. The savings in money alone would seem to justify the experiments;

One of the sea lions trained by Naval Undersea Center animal behaviorists returns to the rubber boat after a successful recovery of an object from the sea floor.

the Navy estimates that it saves about $2,000 per recovery by using sea lions instead of human divers.

If Turk and Fatman can perform such feats, what other underwater tasks may they and their fellow pinnipeds perform someday?

Based on findings of the Sea Mammal Motivational Institute (Seamamm) in the Florida Keys, the answer seems to be: plenty. They might recover objects lost at sea, locate ships and boats lost in storms, function as lifeguards, perhaps even work with humans in underwater construction projects.

Seamamm conducts its studies in an open environment. There are no holding tanks or fences, not even leashes to restrain the animals. Researchers have found that seals and sea lions won't swim away under these conditions if they are shown extraordinary care and affection by their handlers. Research with several pinnipeds at Seamamm has shown that the animals will develop an unusual rapport with certain trainers, responding eagerly to their approach.

One such case involved a year-old harbor seal named Rocky and a handler named Amanda Matthews. After training, Rocky became so accustomed to other humans at the Florida base of Seamamm, that he paid little attention to them. But whenever Miss Matthews approached, he would quickly arouse himself from sleep and drag himself eagerly toward her on his flippers.

Seamamm researchers now believe that pinnipeds have several ways of identifying specific humans to whom they have become accustomed. Rocky, for instance, apparently identified Miss Matthews by the sound of her footfall. Bob Horstman, another trainer, believes that seals also establish identification by the human's breath.

Established in 1970, Seamamm is located in an isolated mangrove swamp on Key Largo in the Florida Keys. It is connected to the Atlantic Ocean by a deep, clear creek. Experiments in the open Atlantic and the Gulf of Mexico are conducted aboard a 65-foot boat, the *Explorer II*. Test animals such as Rocky are not carried to the research area aboard the boat, however; they swim alongside without a leash or tether of any kind.

Besides Rocky, Seamamm animals include Vicky, a two-year-old California sea lion; a seven-year-old female sea lion named Tinkerbelle; and Diana, a fur seal captured in the Pribilof Islands near Alaska.

Theoretically, Seamamm's staff believes that animals such as these might become the nucleus of a breeding herd of pinnipeds which could serve man in a free but controlled state. As man continues to explore the sea, pinnipeds born of this "work herd" would be trained and available for a number of tasks.

To explore this possibility, Horstman has taught Rocky to "rescue" his thirteen-year-old son who pretends to be drowning. Commanded to save the boy, Rocky tows a flotation ring to the "drowning" site and pulls the youngster back to the dock.

Horstman, director of Seamamm, believes that pinnipeds might also be taught to herd fish into nets. He and other researchers have noted that although sea lions are their predators, fish often tend to gather in schools behind swimming sea lions, following them long distances. The fish do not seem wary of the sea lions and with training, pinnipeds can be taught to leave fish alone even if they are hungry.

Various reward systems are used for Seamamm's animals. Rocky and Tinkerbelle respond best to mackerel. Vicky, on the other hand, has been taught to respond to being patted on the head; if she has not performed well, she is not patted. Although seals apparently do not like to be patted, sea lions seem to enjoy it as much as dogs and cats.

Seamamm is a private research institution, whose costs are paid by private donations and grants. The Naval Undersea

Center is financed by government funds. As research facilities they are but two examples—one private, the other public—of man's increased interest in pinnipeds, and in searching for ways that they may share man's interest in exploring and working underwater. Records kept at both NUC and Seamamm of seal-sea lion behavior are, in return, providing scientists with clues as to how humans can assist the pinnipeds.

Detailed journals kept over the last several years provide valuable data not only on how pinnipeds swim, play, eat, reproduce, and react to man's presence, but also on factors that affect their health. A sudden, unexpected loss of appetite might indicate an illness, for instance, which human handlers would diagnose and treat. On the other hand, the information gathered over a long period of time with many animals might better establish how, and at what time of year, pinnipeds do not eat at all.

This would assist human trainers in determining which periods in the pinnipeds' annual life cycle are best for training, and at which times they should be left alone.

In the recently accelerated studies of the world's seals and sea lions, man has learned considerably more about them than during the century or so that he slaughtered them indiscriminately and nearly wiped out some species.

Yet even the strictest controls on seal hunting are not enough to save them if other dangers are ignored. Pesticide poisons and other toxic chemicals, for instance, have been involved in the deaths of some of these highly susceptible animals. According to a study of the Naval Undersea Center, hundreds of sea lion pups have died since 1968 on the Channel Islands off the coast of Southern California alone; although pesticides were not the only cause, they were found to be a significant factor. In a recent two-year period, 1,032 dead sea lion pups were counted on just two of the Channel Islands, and close examination indicated that only a few had died from being crushed or other causes common to pinniped colonies.

Man's increasing activities along the world's coastlines are undoubtedly another adverse influence. Despite their clownish, friendly ways, most seals and sea lions in the wild are wary of humans, especially at breeding time. Seamamm researchers found, as an example, that test animals responded to their training far more readily at the isolated Key Largo site than at a previous one that was frequently crowded with human visitors.

But perhaps the most important key to the survival of the highly adapted, fin-footed animals of the world's oceans will be more of the serious research that only fairly recently has begun. The information that such study is disclosing doubtless will prove of immense value to man, too, as he continues to explore the sea.

Scientific Names
of Seals and Sea Lions

Following are the scientific names given to each of the seals and sea lions; excluding the walrus, they are all of the pinnipeds. The first part of the name is the *genus*. The second part is the *species*.

TRUE SEALS—FAMILY PHOCIDAE

SUBFAMILY: CYSTOPHORINAE

Southern elephant seal	*Mirounga leonina*
Northern elephant seal	*Mirounga augustirotris*
Bladdernose (or hooded) seal	*Cystophora cristata*

SUBFAMILY: PHOCINAE

Common (or harbor) seal	*Phoca vitulina*
Gray seal	*Halichoerus grypus*
Bearded seal	*Erignathus barbatus*
Ringed seal	*Pusa hispada*
Caspian seal	*Pusa caspica*
Baikal seal	*Pusa sibirica*
Harp seal	*Pagophilus groenlandicus*
Ribbon (or banded) seal	*Histriophoca fasciata*

SUBFAMILY: LOBODONTINAE
  Leopard seal   *Hydrurga leptonyx*
  Weddell seal   *Leptonychotes weddelli*
  Ross seal   *Ommatophoca rossi*
  Crabeater seal   *Lobodon carcinophagus*

SUBFAMILY: MONACHINAE
  Mediterranean monk seal   *Monachus monachus*
  Hawaiian monk seal   *Monachus schauinsland*
  Caribbean (or West Indian)   *Monachua tropicalus*
     monk seal

EARED SEALS—FAMILY OTARIIDAE

Northern (or Pribilof or Alaskan) *Callorhinus ursinus*
   fur seal
Southern fur seal   *Arctocephalus australis*
Guadalupe fur seal   *Arctocephalus philippi*
South African (or Cape)   *Arctocephalus pusillus*
   fur seal
Australian fur seal   *Arctocephalus doriferus*
Tasmanian fur seal   *Arctocephalus tasmanicus*
New Zealand fur seal   *Arctocephalus forsteri*
Kerguelen fur seal   *Arctocephalus tropicalis*
Steller's (or northern)   *Eumetopias jubatus*
   sea lion
California sea lion   *Zalophus californianus*
Southern sea lion   *Otaria byronia*
Australian sea lion   *Neophoca cinerea*
Hooker's sea lion   *Phocarctos hookeri*

UNIVERSITY SCHOOL LIBRARY
UNIVERSITY OF WYOMING

Index

(Page numbers in **boldface** are those on which illustrations appear.)

79